Don't be afraid
to be you
Do different

Do Different

Written by
Mya Wilson

Illustrated by
Jarell D. Wilson

1

Printed in the United States of America. The contents of this book are the sole original creation of the author and illustrator and are protected under US Copyright laws. No part of this book may be reproduced, stored in or introduced into a retrieval system, or transmitted in any form, by any means (electronically, mechanical, photocopy, recording, or otherwise) without the expressed written consent of the copyright owner. For information regarding permission, write to Mya Wilson at Cousin Connections Publishing, 40 West 116th Street Suite A 716 New York, NY 10026 or email Mya Wilson at cousinconnections@gmail.com

Printed in the United States of America

Published by:
Cousin Connections Publishing
40 West 116th Street
New York, NY 10026

ISBN: 978-1522846093

Printed by Create Space

We dedicate this book to our grandfather "Poppie" and our great aunt "Auntie".
-MW and JDW

I dedicate this book to my grandmother, Ethel Hassell. I know if you were still here you'd be telling everyone "You know my granddaughter wrote another book!"
Love you Grandma!
-MW

<u>Author's Note:</u>

In this story the character, Ayodele, has a skin condition called vitiligo. Vitiligo is a condition in which your skin loses it's color. This happens when the skin cells stop making color, which causes slowly growing white patches of different shapes to appear on the skin. It usually starts as small spots in different areas on the body and become larger with time. There is no cure for vitiligo. The goal of treatment is to stop or slow the progression of the white spots. For someone who has vitiligo, these changes in the skin can result in stress and worries about how they look.

Both our grandfather and great aunt experienced vitiligo. It was important that one of our books involved Nasir learning the importance of accepting and honoring the uniqueness of people everywhere. So we chose to create a character with a different personality, but who is also different in appearance and gender.

3

One day Nasir's class got quite the surprise.
Ms. Marshall announced a new girl had arrived.

Good morning class, let's welcome our new student Ayodele!

4

"Ayodele is her name
and shy she may seem."

5

"But let's welcome her to our classroom team!"

Good morning class, let's welcome our new Ayodele!

6

Nasir thought...*Ayodele?*
What kind of name could that be?!
Nasir wondered and looked awkwardly.

7

By the end of the week,
He realized Ayodele lived on the same street.

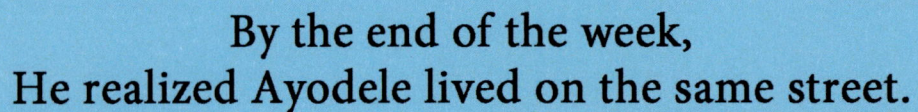

He saw her almost everyday.
Everything she did was done in such a different way.

9

Nasir told his brother Tre
as they walked to school one day...
"Every morning Ayodele says 'Good morning' so loud,
it always startles the whole class crowd!"

Good Morning!!

10

Tre just replied and said...
"Do different Nasir
and soon you will see,
being different shows
how great people can be!"

11

That night after dinner
Nasir told Momma Nae he was the math drill winner...

But then, he went on and on
about how all Ayodele did,
seemed so wrong.

12

"Ayodele has a blue and green racer bike
and she likes to go on nature hikes!"

13

"At recess she waves her Trinidad flag.
Sometimes I think she's such a brag."

14

All Momma Nae replied was...
"Do different Nasir
and soon you will see,
being different shows
how great people can be!"

= Math Drill %
+ WINNER -

15

On Saturday, Nasir and his sister walked to karate.
He told her how Ayodele acted in such a different way.
"She wears a backpack with a big rainbow flower.
Patting her hair saying she has puff power."

Puff Power!

16

His sister only replied...
"Do different Nasir
and soon you will see,
being different shows
how great people can be!"

17

That night,
Nasir went to Grandma Hattie
and tried to explain.
The things Ayodele does
just isn't the same.

But Grandma Hattie stopped him and said,
"There is something I need you to understand son,
being friends with someone who is different from you
can actually be fun!"

18

Nasir thought to himself...*she is just so different I can't see how she could possibly be friends with me.*

19

The next day they had art class at school,
Ayodele told Nasir his drawing was cool.
Confused that she was interested in the same thing as him.
Nasir never imagined them having something in common.

Cool drawing!!

20

That Friday she needed a partner to
go on a nature hike.
Nasir just knew
that wouldn't be something he'd like.

21

But he thought and thought like he often did.
Remembering the words that he'd heard repeated...

22

Do different Nasir
and soon you will see,
being different shows
how great people can be!

The adventures to come he wouldn't know,
but at that moment he decided to go.

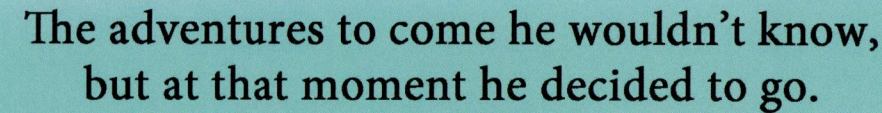

What an afternoon filled with fun.
Nasir hoped it would never be done.

24

Great sights, interesting insects and things to see.
Nasir had no idea how much fun a nature hike could be!
Nasir was glad that he listened to the words that were stuck in his head...
and was pleased that he decided to act on what each family member said.

Trying something different,
and making friends with someone new...
is one of the most exciting things
you could probably ever do!
So just because someone looks, thinks or acts differently...

Do different to find out
how great different people can be!

About the Author and Illustrator

Mya and Jarell are first cousins and have been close since they were small. When they were young they planned to create a comic book together. Mya Wilson was raised in Harlem, New York and is currently a teacher in New York City. She has been teaching for many years, and enjoys reading to her students more than anything else. Jarell D. Wilson was born and raised in Long Island, New York. Since his early years, Jarell has been drawing and finding ways to express his creativity through art. This is their second collaboration. They hope to create more amazing children's stories. Be sure to check out their other book "Love You Still".

About "Love You Still":

Meet Nasir...He is starting to think that everyone is going to be angry with him forever for all of the things that he does wrong. But Nasir soon learns an important lesson about the adults and older people who take care of him. Read to find out what Nasir and all children should remember when they have made a mistake or done something wrong.